AMERICA'S SONGS

GOD *Bless* AMERICA

Cavendish Square
New York

STEPHANIE LUNDQUIST-ARORA

Published in 2020 by Cavendish Square Publishing, LLC
243 5th Avenue, Suite 136, New York, NY 10016

First Edition

Website: cavendishsq.com

Library of Congress Cataloging-in-Publication Data

Names: Lundquist-Arora, Stephanie, author.
Title: God bless America / Stephanie Lundquist-Arora.
Description: First edition. | New York : Cavendish Square, 2020. | Series: America's songs | Includes bibliographical references and index. | Identifiers: LCCN 2018057898 (print) | LCCN 2018058608 (ebook) | ISBN 9781502648686 (ebook) | ISBN 9781502648679 (library bound) | ISBN 9781502648655 (pbk.) | ISBN 9781502648662 (6 pack)
Subjects: LCSH: Berlin, Irving, 1888-1989. God bless America--Juvenile literature.
Classification: LCC ML3930.B446 (ebook) | LCC ML3930.B446 L85 2020 (print) | DDC 782.42/15990973--dc23
LC record available at https://lccn.loc.gov/2018057898

Editorial Director: David McNamara
Editor: Lauren Miller
Copy Editor: Nathan Heidelberger
Associate Art Director: Alan Sliwinski
Designer: Joe Parenteau
Production Coordinator: Karol Szymczuk
Photo Research: J8 Media

The photographs in this book are used by permission and through the courtesy of: Cover Straight 8 Photography/Shutterstock.com; p. 4 JohnnyA 123/iStock/Getty Images; p. 6 transcribed by Dr. Nathan Heidelberger; p. 7, 12, 20 Bettmann/Getty Images; p. 8 Everett Collection/Newscom; p. 9 Joseph Sohm/Shutterstock.com; p. 10 Xavier Ascanio/Shutterstock.com; p. 14 New York Times Co./Getty Images; p. 15 Pictorial Parade/Getty Images; p. 17 Bettmann Archive/Corbis/Getty Images; p. 18 Hulton Archive/Getty Images; p. 19 Everett Collection; p. 22 Douglas Graham/Roll Call/Getty Images; p. 24 Robert Giroux/Getty Images; p. 26 Keith Bedford/The Boston Globe/Getty Images; p. 27 Elsa/Getty Images.

Printed in the United States of America

CONTENTS

Seeing a beautiful American landscape sometimes makes people think of the song "God Bless America." They are happy for the trees, mountains, and blue skies.

CHAPTER 1

The Unofficial National Anthem

"God Bless America" is one of the United States' favorite songs. It is also a **patriotic** song. That means people think of the song when they think about the United States. It has been a popular song since 1938. A famous singer named Kate Smith first sang the song. She sang it on her radio show on November 10, 1938.

God Bless America

Lyrics and Music by Irving Berlin

Famous singer Kate Smith sang "God Bless America" often on her radio show.

She said it was "one of the most beautiful **compositions** ever written. A song that will never die."

When Americans heard it, many loved the song. It became an instant success. From November 1938 to January 1941, Kate Smith sang "God Bless America" almost every week on her radio show. The song grew even more famous.

FACT

"God Bless America" grew so popular in the late 1930s that many Americans wanted it to be the county's national anthem. "The Star-Spangled Banner" became the national anthem in 1931.

Presidential Awards

In the 1940s, 1950s, and 1970s, three US presidents gave the song's writer, Irving Berlin, special awards for the song. In 1945, President Harry S. Truman gave

Irving Berlin (*center*) shakes General George C. Marshall's hand after receiving the Medal for Merit in 1945. Berlin's wife, Ellin, is by his side.

him the Army Medal for Merit. President Dwight D. Eisenhower gave him the Congressional Gold Medal for "God Bless America" in 1954. In 1977, President Gerald Ford gave the Medal of Freedom to him. The Medal of Freedom was earned because Berlin's music helped people connect to their "fondest dreams" and "deepest emotions."

FACT

In 1940, Irving Berlin started the God Bless America Fund. It gives money to the Boy Scouts and Girl Scouts every time "God Bless America" is **licensed**.

The Boy Scouts of America have a special connection to "God Bless America."

Today, “God Bless America” is still important. It continues to be popular and loved. It has helped many people through difficult times. It continues to help people today. It is also a popular song to sing at special times or when remembering other people who have died.

“God Bless America” mentions beautiful American scenery—oceans, mountains, and prairies. Here, sunlight bathes mountains and a valley, making a breathtaking view.

The Meaning of "God Bless America"

"God Bless America" is a prayer that asks God to protect the country always. The phrase "through the night" asks for protection in darkness, or difficult times. The words "from the mountains to the prairies / to the oceans white with foam" ask to protect the nation from end to end. "A light from above" means a light God uses to guide the people.

The second line of the song, "Land that I love," meant a lot to Irving Berlin. Berlin came from another country. He wrote the song to thank God and the country for giving him and his family a home.

Words to Know

foam A mass of small bubbles formed on or in liquid.
prairies Large open areas of grassland.

Irving Berlin sits at the piano in the 1940s. He enjoyed playing piano and practicing the songs he wrote.

CHAPTER 2

The Song Goes National

"God Bless America" was written by Irving Berlin. Berlin was an immigrant. In 1893, Berlin was five years old. He and his family had to leave Russia. They were in danger. They were Jewish, and some people in Russia did not want them living there. They moved to the

United States. As he grew up, Berlin remembered his mother saying "God bless America" because she was so glad she and her family had a safe place to live. These words would inspire the song.

Irving Berlin, a young man in 1922, poses for the camera.

Irving Berlin's Path to Learning to Play the Piano

After Berlin's father died, Berlin needed to earn money to help his family. Though he was just thirteen years old, he stopped going to school. He had many jobs. First he sold newspapers. Then he sang on busy street corners.

> **FACT**
> Irving Berlin's style of music is called pop (or popular) music.

Later, he got a job as a singing waiter. He learned to play the piano and started writing his own songs.

Irving Berlin: Citizen and Soldier

In 1918, Berlin became a US **citizen**. Back then, the United States was in a war. The war was called World War I. Many countries fought in World War I. Male citizens of the United States had to fight in the war. Berlin was **drafted** into the US Army. While in the army, he continued writing songs. He wrote a funny musical

This solider rushes into a fight during World War I.

to raise money for the soldiers. It was called *Yip! Yip! Yaphank*. "God Bless America" was written for this musical. It was too serious to use in the funny play, though.

"God Bless America" Becomes Famous

In 1938, Berlin went to London, England. When he was there, he thought another war would happen in Europe. When he returned to the United States, Berlin wanted to write a song that helped people think of peace. He remembered "God Bless America." It was the perfect song. He made some changes to it. A few days later, radio show host Kate Smith asked him for a song to play on her radio show. Berlin gave her "God Bless America." She sang it on the radio on November 10, 1938. She made the song a famous **ballad**.

"God Bless America" During World War II

The song became more popular after the United States entered World War II in 1941. Times were difficult. Many Americans sang the prayer that often played on the radio. They liked how comforting it was.

Women gather around a radio during World War II. Radio was one of the main ways people enjoyed stories and received news in the 1930s and 1940s.

FACT

"God Bless America" was first performed the day after a horrible event called Kristallnacht. That was when some people in Germany and other parts of Europe destroyed Jewish buildings and businesses. Kristallnacht made "God Bless America" a song of war rather than peace.

On November 10, 1938, people stare at one of many stores that was destroyed during Kristallnacht the night before.

During World War II, Berlin volunteered for the army. He wrote a show called *This Is the Army*. In 1943, it was made into a movie. It starred Ronald Reagan. Reagan was later the fortieth president of the United States. "God Bless America" played in this movie. It was the first time the song had been played in a movie.

This scene shows Ronald Reagan (*left*) acting in the movie *This Is the Army*.

President Dwight D. Eisenhower gave Berlin an award in 1954. The award was a Congressional Gold Medal. It was given to him because "God Bless America" had helped America through World War II. The song has been a song of America ever since.

President Dwight D. Eisenhower, pictured here in the White House, gave Irving Berlin an acclaimed award in 1954.

Timeline

- **1893** Five-year-old Irving Berlin moves with his family to New York. They left Russia for their safety.
- **1914–1918** World War I happens.
- **1918** Irving Berlin becomes a US citizen. He is drafted into the US Army. There he creates the musical *Yip! Yip! Yaphank* to raise money for the soldiers. He writes "God Bless America" but does not use it.
- **1938** Berlin updates the words to "God Bless America." It airs on the eve of **Armistice Day**. One day before, Kristallacht happens.
- **1939** World War II begins.
- **1943** A movie called *This Is the Army* plays "God Bless America" in it.
- **1945** World War II ends.
- **1954** President Eisenhower awards Irving Berlin the Congressional Gold Medal for "God Bless America."

Members of the US Congress sing "God Bless America" on the steps of the Capitol Building after the terrorist attacks of September 11, 2001.

CHAPTER 3

From Baseball Stadiums to the Steps of Congress

Today, "God Bless America" continues to be a song about patriotism, comfort, and hope. Its popularity did not decrease after World War II. In fact, it has become more popular ever since.

It has brought people hope in the darkest times of US history.

"God Bless America" Brings Comfort

On September 11, 2001, "God Bless America" became a song that brought all Americans together. On that sad day, two planes hit the World Trade Center in New York City. Another plane crashed into the Pentagon in Washington, DC. Later that day, members of the US **Congress** sang "God Bless America" on

The Twin Towers of the World Trade Center in New York City billow with smoke after two planes crashed into them on September 11, 2001.

the Capitol Building steps. On September 23, 2001, when the Kansas City Chiefs hosted the New York Giants for their first professional football game since the attack, both teams held hands while "God Bless America" played. Americans came together to raise money for the victims of September 11. At one of these benefits, famous singer Celine Dion performed "God Bless America."

> **FACT**
> Irving Berlin died in 1989. He was 101 years old. Then president George H. W. Bush gave a speech about Berlin. He said that Berlin had "touch[ed] the soul of a nation."

Today's Uses

Today, "God Bless America" is played usually around the Fourth of July. Many churches play it during their Independence Day services. Bands and orchestras play it in Fourth of July ceremonies and parades.

Famous singers and performers also sing the song at these special celebrations. On July 4, 2011, for example, Martina McBride sang "God Bless America" with the Boston Pops Orchestra.

Fourth of July celebrations often include singing or playing patriotic songs like "God Bless America."

"God Bless America" is a song that will always help people. It will help people comfort each other in difficult times. It will give strength and hope to people who need it. It will continue to bring peace to many. It will always be a song of America.

FACT

Berlin wrote more than 1,500 songs during his lifetime, but he donated any money for "God Bless America" to the Boy Scouts of America and Girl Scouts of America.

"God Bless America" at Sports Events

"God Bless America" has been played at many sporting events throughout the years. On October 11, 1973, Kate Smith performed "God Bless America" at a Philadelphia Flyers hockey game, and then again at the Stanley Cup playoff game against the Boston Bruins on May 12, 1974. Today, the New York Yankees also play "God Bless America" at every home game. At many baseball games, the spectators sing "God Bless America" during the seventh-inning stretch. Many other famous singers have performed the song at sports games and other popular events.

Marc Anthony sings the song at the MLB All-Star Game in 2013.

GLOSSARY

Armistice Day The day that celebrates the end of World War I.

ballad A song with a lot of meaning.

citizen A person who is born into a country or someone who decides to become a member of a country by studying and passing a special test about the country.

compositions Songs.

Congress People who work for a country and make rules for the country. They represent the people living in the country too.

drafted To make someone fight in a war.

licensed Giving permission to print or use a work of art, such as a song.

patriotic Showing support for one's country.

FIND OUT MORE

Books

Churnin, Nancy. *Irving Berlin: The Immigrant Boy Who Made America Sing*. Berkeley, CA: Creston Books, 2018.

Kimmelman, Leslie. *Write On, Irving Berlin!* Ann Arbor, MI: Sleeping Bear Press, 2018.

Nuchi, Adah. *God Bless America: The Story of an Immigrant Named Irving Berlin*. New York: Disney Hyperion, 2018.

Websites

Biography: Irving Berlin

https://www.biography.com/people/irving-berlin-9209473

This website gives information about Irving Berlin, the man who wrote "God Bless America." It tells his life story, explores his accomplishments and friends, and notes more of the songs he is known for composing.

Irving Berlin Website

http://www.irvingberlin.com

This is the official website of Irving Berlin. It contains a detailed biography about him, information about his songs, and online sources where you can listen to his music today.

Video

God Bless America: Kate Smith's First Radio Performance

https://www.youtube.com/watch?v=b1rKQReqJZg

This is the original radio broadcast performance of "God Bless America" by Irving Berlin, as introduced by Kate Smith on November 10, 1938.

INDEX

Page numbers in **boldface** refer to images. Entries in **boldface** are glossary terms.

ABOUT THE AUTHOR

Stephanie Lundquist-Arora has master's degrees in political science and public administration. She lives in Northern Virginia with her husband and three sons. She enjoys listening to "God Bless America" and many other songs. When not writing, she likes traveling with her family, jogging, reading, and trying new foods.